bush
PUBLISHING
& associates

PRESENTED TO

FROM

ON

THE CHAMPION
PRAYER PARTNER
For Men

The Victory is in the Answer

David Harrelson

bush
PUBLISHING
& associates

Unless otherwise indicated, all Scripture quotations are taken from the New King James Version of the Bible, copyright © 1979, 1980, 1982, Thomas Nelson, Inc., Publishers.
All Scripture quotations marked KJV are taken from the King James Version of the Bible.

THE CHAMPION PRAYER PARTNER FOR MEN OF GOD
By David Harrelson
Hardcover ISBN: 978-1-944566-50-0
Softcover ISBN: 978-1--944566-51-7
Copyright ©2023 by David Harrelson

Bush Publishing & Associates, LLC books may be ordered at everywhere and at Amazon.com
For further information, please contact:
Bush Publishing & Associates
Tulsa, Oklahoma
www.bushpublishing.com

Printed in the United States of America.

No portion of this book may be used or reproduced by any means: graphic, electronic or mechanical, including photocopying, recording, taping, or by any information storage retrieval system, without the written permission of the publisher, except in the case of brief quotations embodied in critical articles and reviews.

I dedicate this book to my family, starting with my wife, who has always believed in me and encouraged me to do things well beyond my capabilities.

Secondly, to all the kids that God has blessed me with. Whether biological, adopted, or fostered, they are my true inspiration. I cherish watching them grow into men and women, being a part of their successes and failures, and having the privilege and the responsibility of guiding it all. Ultimately, having them teach me to be a better person as they venture off to pursue their goals and dreams and witnessing how their faith and prayer play a huge role in their life, is the legacy I am most proud of.

Train up a child in the way he should go, and when he is old he will not depart from it.
Proverbs 22:6

HOW TO USE YOUR PRAYER PARTNER

By choosing to use your champion prayer partner, you've made one of the best decisions a man of God could make. Having a record of God's faithfulness is by far one of the best ways to supercharge your faith. Use these simple steps below as a guide to help you get the most out of your Champion prayer partner.

MAKE A RECORD

1). Keep your Champion prayer partner accessible and use it often. Record all of your prayer requests, large and small. Even if you don't have time to fill out the entire request page, at least fill in the Date and the " I am praying for" section and you can fill in the rest when you have more time. Use the notes and pictures page to record additional information about your prayer request. Place before and after pictures of what you're praying for and pictures of what God provided.

STAND ON SCRIPTURE

2). Select one to three scriptures of your own or from the back of your prayer partner, that you can memorize and speak over your prayer request. Write them down in the "scriptures, I am standing on" section of your prayer request page.

CHECK YOUR FAITH

3). After you have filled out your prayer request page and selected the scriptures you are going to stand upon, accurately and honestly select a faith level number between 1 and 10 at the top of the page. This is a visual reminder of where you believe your faith level is for this specific prayer request. This will become a powerful tool for you over time.

RECORD PROGRESS

4). Anytime a change occurs regarding your prayer request write it down in the "updates" section.

DOCUMENT YOUR RESPONSE

5). When God answers your prayer, use the "my response was" section and write down exactly what you felt and what you did at the moment you realized your prayer had been answered. Lastly, you can place a big X in the answered prayer box at the top of the "Notes and Pictures" page, and you will watch your faith increase exponentially for every X you record.

MAKING OF A CHAMPION

After years of serving as a youth pastor, I found myself leading an unusually active and passionate youth group of mostly mid to older teens. I had noticed that this particular group was very active in their prayer life and loved to pray for the needs of people. I began to see God consistently move through them in profound and miraculous ways. With each answered prayer, you could see exponential growth in the group's individual and group faith. It seemed that God was answering every prayer request, large and small, just to prove a point to the youth that God the Father was real. To this day I believe that God wanted the faith of our youth group to be so strong that not one would ever walk away from their faith. Just to name a few, we saw our youth bus donated, salvations increased, families restored, finances grew, stolen vehicles returned, jobs provided, promotions given, home loans approved, people's lives extended, projects funded, and pets healed. We even witnessed a stage 4 cancer patient get a cancer free report with the clear x-rays to prove it, one week after our youth group prayed.

The move of God was so strong and obvious that adults began attending our youth services and requesting the youth group to pray for them. One Sunday, as I was on my way to preach a youth service, God prompted me to stop and buy about 30 small spiral notebooks. When I arrived at the service, I handed everyone a notebook. I told them to begin recording their prayer requests by date with descriptions and to leave a space between requests to record the date when the prayer was answered. Amazingly, most of them started doing it and they kept the notebooks on them, in their cars, and in their school backpacks. They were using them because they could see visual proof that God was hearing their prayers and often moving quickly to manifest their prayers into reality. The cheap little plain notebooks had become a major faith builder, encouraging them with visual evidence of God's faithfulness every time they looked at the notebook. God had taken these little notebooks and used them as a huge faith builder for these amazing teenagers. Little did I know that these notebooks would become the basic idea behind the Champion Prayer Partner.

THE CHAMPION

MY FAITH LEVEL   1 - 2 - 3 - 4 - 5 - 6 - 7 - 8 - 9 - 10

DATE

I AM ASKING GOD FOR
___
___
___
___
___
___

SCRIPTURES I AM STANDING ON
___
___
___
___
___
___

UPDATES
___
___
___
___
___
___

MY RESPONSE TO GOD'S ANSWER
___
___
___
___
___
___

So Jesus answered and said to them, "Have faith in God."
Mark 11:12

NOTES AND PICTURES

PRAYER ANSWERED

For where two or three are gathered together in My name, I am there in the midst of them.
Matthew 18:20

MY FAITH LEVEL   1 - 2 - 3 - 4 - 5 - 6 - 7 - 8 - 9 - 10

DATE

I AM ASKING GOD FOR
_____
_____
_____
_____
_____

SCRIPTURES I AM STANDING ON
_____
_____
_____
_____
_____

UPDATES
_____
_____
_____
_____
_____

MY RESPONSE TO GOD'S ANSWER
_____
_____
_____
_____
_____

So Jesus answered and said to them, "Have faith in God."
Mark 11:12

NOTES AND PICTURES

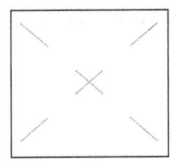

PRAYER
ANSWERED

For where two or three are gathered together in My name, I am there in the midst of them.
Matthew 18:20

MY FAITH LEVEL 1 - 2 - 3 - 4 - 5 - 6 - 7 - 8 - 9 - 10

DATE

I AM ASKING GOD FOR
_____
_____
_____
_____
_____
_____

SCRIPTURES I AM STANDING ON
_____
_____
_____
_____
_____
_____

UPDATES
_____
_____
_____
_____
_____
_____

MY RESPONSE TO GOD'S ANSWER
_____
_____
_____
_____
_____
_____

So Jesus answered and said to them, "Have faith in God."
Mark 11:12

NOTES AND PICTURES

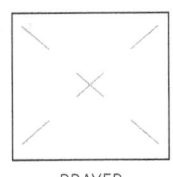
PRAYER ANSWERED

For where two or three are gathered together in My name, I am there in the midst of them.
Matthew 18:20

MY FAITH LEVEL   1 - 2 - 3 - 4 - 5 - 6 - 7 - 8 - 9 - 10

DATE

I AM ASKING GOD FOR

_____
_____
_____
_____
_____

SCRIPTURES I AM STANDING ON

_____
_____
_____
_____
_____

UPDATES

_____
_____
_____
_____
_____

MY RESPONSE TO GOD'S ANSWER

_____
_____
_____
_____
_____

So Jesus answered and said to them, "Have faith in God."
Mark 11:12

NOTES AND PICTURES

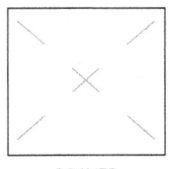
PRAYER ANSWERED

For where two or three are gathered together in My name, I am there in the midst of them.
Matthew 18:20

MY FAITH LEVEL 1 - 2 - 3 - 4 - 5 - 6 - 7 - 8 - 9 - 10

DATE

I AM ASKING GOD FOR
___
___
___
___
___

SCRIPTURES I AM STANDING ON
___
___
___
___
___

UPDATES
___
___
___
___
___

MY RESPONSE TO GOD'S ANSWER
___
___
___
___
___

So Jesus answered and said to them, "Have faith in God."
Mark 11:12

NOTES AND PICTURES

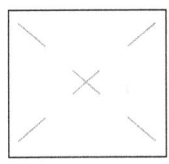
PRAYER ANSWERED

For where two or three are gathered together in My name, I am there in the midst of them.
Matthew 18:20

MY FAITH LEVEL   1 - 2 - 3 - 4 - 5 - 6 - 7 - 8 - 9 - 10

DATE

I AM ASKING GOD FOR

___
___
___
___
___
___

SCRIPTURES I AM STANDING ON

___
___
___
___
___
___

UPDATES

___
___
___
___
___
___

MY RESPONSE TO GOD'S ANSWER

___
___
___
___
___
___

So Jesus answered and said to them, "Have faith in God."
Mark 11:12

NOTES AND PICTURES

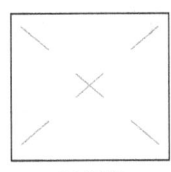

PRAYER ANSWERED

For where two or three are gathered together in My name, I am there in the midst of them.
Matthew 18:20

MY FAITH LEVEL   1 - 2 - 3 - 4 - 5 - 6 - 7 - 8 - 9 - 10

DATE

I AM ASKING GOD FOR

_____
_____
_____
_____
_____
_____

SCRIPTURES I AM STANDING ON

_____
_____
_____
_____
_____
_____

UPDATES

_____
_____
_____
_____
_____
_____

MY RESPONSE TO GOD'S ANSWER

_____
_____
_____
_____
_____
_____

So Jesus answered and said to them, "Have faith in God."
Mark 11:12

NOTES AND PICTURES

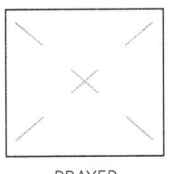
PRAYER
ANSWERED

For where two or three are gathered together in My name, I am there in the midst of them.
Matthew 18:20

MY FAITH LEVEL   1 - 2 - 3 - 4 - 5 - 6 - 7 - 8 - 9 - 10

DATE

I AM ASKING GOD FOR

SCRIPTURES I AM STANDING ON

UPDATES

MY RESPONSE TO GOD'S ANSWER

So Jesus answered and said to them, "Have faith in God."
Mark 11:12

NOTES AND PICTURES

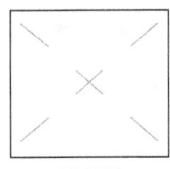

PRAYER
ANSWERED

For where two or three are gathered together in My name, I am there in the midst of them.
Matthew 18:20

MY FAITH LEVEL   1 - 2 - 3 - 4 - 5 - 6 - 7 - 8 - 9 - 10

DATE

I AM ASKING GOD FOR
_____
_____
_____
_____
_____
_____

SCRIPTURES I AM STANDING ON
_____
_____
_____
_____
_____
_____

UPDATES
_____
_____
_____
_____
_____
_____

MY RESPONSE TO GOD'S ANSWER
_____
_____
_____
_____
_____
_____

So Jesus answered and said to them, "Have faith in God."
Mark 11:12

NOTES AND PICTURES

PRAYER
ANSWERED

For where two or three are gathered together in My name, I am there in the midst of them.
Matthew 18:20

MY FAITH LEVEL 1 - 2 - 3 - 4 - 5 - 6 - 7 - 8 - 9 - 10

DATE

I AM ASKING GOD FOR

_____
_____
_____
_____
_____
_____

SCRIPTURES I AM STANDING ON

_____
_____
_____
_____
_____
_____

UPDATES

_____
_____
_____
_____
_____

MY RESPONSE TO GOD'S ANSWER

_____
_____
_____
_____
_____
_____

So Jesus answered and said to them, "Have faith in God."
Mark 11:12

NOTES AND PICTURES

PRAYER
ANSWERED

For where two or three are gathered together in My name, I am there in the midst of them.
Matthew 18:20

MY FAITH LEVEL 1 - 2 - 3 - 4 - 5 - 6 - 7 - 8 - 9 - 10

DATE

I AM ASKING GOD FOR

_____
_____
_____
_____
_____
_____

SCRIPTURES I AM STANDING ON

_____
_____
_____
_____
_____
_____

UPDATES

_____
_____
_____
_____
_____
_____

MY RESPONSE TO GOD'S ANSWER

_____
_____
_____
_____
_____
_____

So Jesus answered and said to them, "Have faith in God."
Mark 11:12

NOTES AND PICTURES

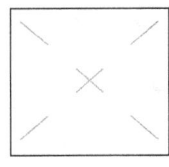

PRAYER
ANSWERED

For where two or three are gathered together in My name, I am there in the midst of them.
Matthew 18:20

MY FAITH LEVEL   1 - 2 - 3 - 4 - 5 - 6 - 7 - 8 - 9 - 10

DATE

I AM ASKING GOD FOR
_____
_____
_____
_____
_____
_____

SCRIPTURES I AM STANDING ON
_____
_____
_____
_____
_____
_____

UPDATES
_____
_____
_____
_____
_____
_____

MY RESPONSE TO GOD'S ANSWER
_____
_____
_____
_____
_____
_____

So Jesus answered and said to them, "Have faith in God."
Mark 11:12

NOTES AND PICTURES

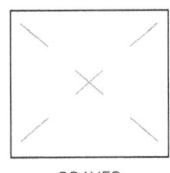

PRAYER
ANSWERED

For where two or three are gathered together in My name, I am there in the midst of them.
Matthew 18:20

MY FAITH LEVEL   1 - 2 - 3 - 4 - 5 - 6 - 7 - 8 - 9 - 10

DATE

I AM ASKING GOD FOR
_____
_____
_____
_____
_____
_____

SCRIPTURES I AM STANDING ON
_____
_____
_____
_____
_____
_____

UPDATES
_____
_____
_____
_____
_____
_____

MY RESPONSE TO GOD'S ANSWER
_____
_____
_____
_____
_____
_____

So Jesus answered and said to them, "Have faith in God."
Mark 11:12

NOTES AND PICTURES

PRAYER
ANSWERED

For where two or three are gathered together in My name, I am there in the midst of them.
Matthew 18:20

MY FAITH LEVEL 1 - 2 - 3 - 4 - 5 - 6 - 7 - 8 - 9 - 10

DATE

I AM ASKING GOD FOR
___
___
___
___
___
___

SCRIPTURES I AM STANDING ON
___
___
___
___
___
___

UPDATES
___
___
___
___
___
___

MY RESPONSE TO GOD'S ANSWER
___
___
___
___
___
___

So Jesus answered and said to them, "Have faith in God."
Mark 11:12

NOTES AND PICTURES

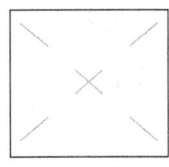

PRAYER
ANSWERED

For where two or three are gathered together in My name, I am there in the midst of them.
Matthew 18:20

MY FAITH LEVEL 1 - 2 - 3 - 4 - 5 - 6 - 7 - 8 - 9 - 10

DATE

I AM ASKING GOD FOR
_____
_____
_____
_____
_____
_____

SCRIPTURES I AM STANDING ON
_____
_____
_____
_____
_____
_____

UPDATES
_____
_____
_____
_____
_____
_____

MY RESPONSE TO GOD'S ANSWER
_____
_____
_____
_____
_____
_____

So Jesus answered and said to them, "Have faith in God."
Mark 11:12

NOTES AND PICTURES

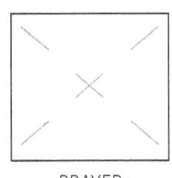

PRAYER ANSWERED

For where two or three are gathered together in My name, I am there in the midst of them.
Matthew 18:20

MY FAITH LEVEL   1 - 2 - 3 - 4 - 5 - 6 - 7 - 8 - 9 - 10

DATE

I AM ASKING GOD FOR

_____
_____
_____
_____
_____
_____

SCRIPTURES I AM STANDING ON

_____
_____
_____
_____
_____
_____

UPDATES

_____
_____
_____
_____
_____

MY RESPONSE TO GOD'S ANSWER

_____
_____
_____
_____
_____

So Jesus answered and said to them, "Have faith in God."
Mark 11:12

NOTES AND PICTURES

PRAYER ANSWERED

For where two or three are gathered together in My name, I am there in the midst of them.
Matthew 18:20

MY FAITH LEVEL 1 - 2 - 3 - 4 - 5 - 6 - 7 - 8 - 9 - 10

DATE

I AM ASKING GOD FOR

SCRIPTURES I AM STANDING ON

UPDATES

MY RESPONSE TO GOD'S ANSWER

So Jesus answered and said to them, "Have faith in God."
Mark 11:12

NOTES AND PICTURES

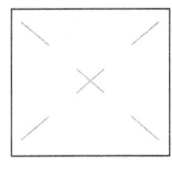

PRAYER
ANSWERED

For where two or three are gathered together in My name, I am there in the midst of them.
Matthew 18:20

MY FAITH LEVEL   1 - 2 - 3 - 4 - 5 - 6 - 7 - 8 - 9 - 10

DATE

I AM ASKING GOD FOR

_____
_____
_____
_____
_____
_____

SCRIPTURES I AM STANDING ON

_____
_____
_____
_____
_____
_____

UPDATES

_____
_____
_____
_____
_____
_____

MY RESPONSE TO GOD'S ANSWER

_____
_____
_____
_____
_____
_____

So Jesus answered and said to them, "Have faith in God."
Mark 11:12

NOTES AND PICTURES

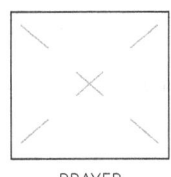

PRAYER ANSWERED

For where two or three are gathered together in My name, I am there in the midst of them.
Matthew 18:20

MY FAITH LEVEL   1 - 2 - 3 - 4 - 5 - 6 - 7 - 8 - 9 - 10

DATE

I AM ASKING GOD FOR
_____
_____
_____
_____
_____
_____

SCRIPTURES I AM STANDING ON
_____
_____
_____
_____
_____
_____

UPDATES
_____
_____
_____
_____
_____
_____

MY RESPONSE TO GOD'S ANSWER
_____
_____
_____
_____
_____
_____

So Jesus answered and said to them, "Have faith in God."
Mark 11:12

NOTES AND PICTURES

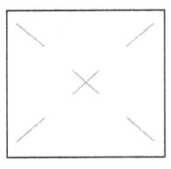
PRAYER ANSWERED

For where two or three are gathered together in My name, I am there in the midst of them.
Matthew 18:20

MY FAITH LEVEL   1 - 2 - 3 - 4 - 5 - 6 - 7 - 8 - 9 - 10

DATE

I AM ASKING GOD FOR
___
___
___
___
___
___

SCRIPTURES I AM STANDING ON
___
___
___
___
___
___

UPDATES
___
___
___
___
___
___

MY RESPONSE TO GOD'S ANSWER
___
___
___
___
___

So Jesus answered and said to them, "Have faith in God."
Mark 11:12

NOTES AND PICTURES

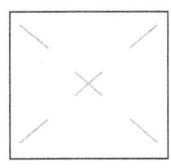

PRAYER
ANSWERED

For where two or three are gathered together in My name, I am there in the midst of them.
Matthew 18:20

MY FAITH LEVEL   1 - 2 - 3 - 4 - 5 - 6 - 7 - 8 - 9 - 10

DATE

I AM ASKING GOD FOR
_____
_____
_____
_____
_____
_____

SCRIPTURES I AM STANDING ON
_____
_____
_____
_____
_____
_____

UPDATES
_____
_____
_____
_____
_____

MY RESPONSE TO GOD'S ANSWER
_____
_____
_____
_____
_____
_____

So Jesus answered and said to them, "Have faith in God."
Mark 11:12

NOTES AND PICTURES

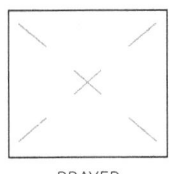

PRAYER
ANSWERED

For where two or three are gathered together in My name, I am there in the midst of them.
Matthew 18:20

MY FAITH LEVEL   1 - 2 - 3 - 4 - 5 - 6 - 7 - 8 - 9 - 10

DATE

I AM ASKING GOD FOR
_____
_____
_____
_____
_____
_____

SCRIPTURES I AM STANDING ON
_____
_____
_____
_____
_____
_____

UPDATES
_____
_____
_____
_____
_____
_____

MY RESPONSE TO GOD'S ANSWER
_____
_____
_____
_____
_____
_____

So Jesus answered and said to them, "Have faith in God."
Mark 11:12

NOTES AND PICTURES

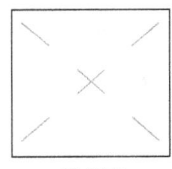
PRAYER ANSWERED

For where two or three are gathered together in My name, I am there in the midst of them.
Matthew 18:20

MY FAITH LEVEL 1 - 2 - 3 - 4 - 5 - 6 - 7 - 8 - 9 - 10

DATE

I AM ASKING GOD FOR

_____
_____
_____
_____
_____

SCRIPTURES I AM STANDING ON

_____
_____
_____
_____
_____

UPDATES

_____
_____
_____
_____
_____

MY RESPONSE TO GOD'S ANSWER

_____
_____
_____
_____
_____

So Jesus answered and said to them, "Have faith in God."
Mark 11:12

NOTES AND PICTURES

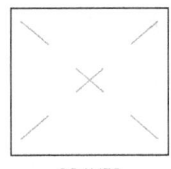

PRAYER
ANSWERED

For where two or three are gathered together in My name, I am there in the midst of them.
Matthew 18:20

MY FAITH LEVEL 1 - 2 - 3 - 4 - 5 - 6 - 7 - 8 - 9 - 10

DATE

I AM ASKING GOD FOR

___
___
___
___
___
___

SCRIPTURES I AM STANDING ON

___
___
___
___
___
___

UPDATES

___
___
___
___
___
___

MY RESPONSE TO GOD'S ANSWER

___
___
___
___
___
___

So Jesus answered and said to them, "Have faith in God."
Mark 11:12

NOTES AND PICTURES

PRAYER
ANSWERED

For where two or three are gathered together in My name, I am there in the midst of them.
Matthew 18:20

MY FAITH LEVEL 1 - 2 - 3 - 4 - 5 - 6 - 7 - 8 - 9 - 10

DATE

I AM ASKING GOD FOR

SCRIPTURES I AM STANDING ON

UPDATES

MY RESPONSE TO GOD'S ANSWER

So Jesus answered and said to them, "Have faith in God."
Mark 11:12

NOTES AND PICTURES

PRAYER ANSWERED

For where two or three are gathered together in My name, I am there in the midst of them.
Matthew 18:20

MY FAITH LEVEL 1 - 2 - 3 - 4 - 5 - 6 - 7 - 8 - 9 - 10

DATE

I AM ASKING GOD FOR
_____
_____
_____
_____
_____
_____

SCRIPTURES I AM STANDING ON
_____
_____
_____
_____
_____
_____

UPDATES
_____
_____
_____
_____
_____

MY RESPONSE TO GOD'S ANSWER
_____
_____
_____
_____
_____
_____

So Jesus answered and said to them, "Have faith in God."
Mark 11:12

NOTES AND PICTURES

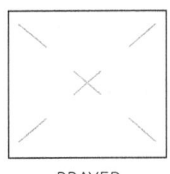

PRAYER
ANSWERED

For where two or three are gathered together in My name, I am there in the midst of them.
Matthew 18:20

MY FAITH LEVEL 1 - 2 - 3 - 4 - 5 - 6 - 7 - 8 - 9 - 10

DATE

I AM ASKING GOD FOR

SCRIPTURES I AM STANDING ON

UPDATES

MY RESPONSE TO GOD'S ANSWER

So Jesus answered and said to them, "Have faith in God."
Mark 11:12

NOTES AND PICTURES

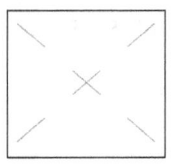
PRAYER ANSWERED

For where two or three are gathered together in My name, I am there in the midst of them.
Matthew 18:20

MY FAITH LEVEL   1 - 2 - 3 - 4 - 5 - 6 - 7 - 8 - 9 - 10

DATE

I AM ASKING GOD FOR

___

SCRIPTURES I AM STANDING ON

___

UPDATES

___

MY RESPONSE TO GOD'S ANSWER

___

So Jesus answered and said to them, "Have faith in God."
Mark 11:12

NOTES AND PICTURES

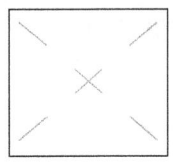

PRAYER
ANSWERED

For where two or three are gathered together in My name, I am there in the midst of them.
Matthew 18:20

MY FAITH LEVEL   1 - 2 - 3 - 4 - 5 - 6 - 7 - 8 - 9 - 10

DATE

I AM ASKING GOD FOR

SCRIPTURES I AM STANDING ON

UPDATES

MY RESPONSE TO GOD'S ANSWER

So Jesus answered and said to them, "Have faith in God."
Mark 11:12

NOTES AND PICTURES

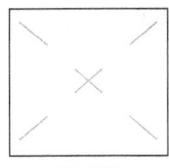

PRAYER
ANSWERED

For where two or three are gathered together in My name, I am there in the midst of them.
Matthew 18:20

MY FAITH LEVEL   1 - 2 - 3 - 4 - 5 - 6 - 7 - 8 - 9 - 10

DATE

I AM ASKING GOD FOR
___
___
___
___
___
___

SCRIPTURES I AM STANDING ON
___
___
___
___
___
___

UPDATES
___
___
___
___
___

MY RESPONSE TO GOD'S ANSWER
___
___
___
___
___
___

So Jesus answered and said to them, "Have faith in God."
Mark 11:12

NOTES AND PICTURES

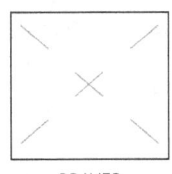
PRAYER ANSWERED

For where two or three are gathered together in My name, I am there in the midst of them.
Matthew 18:20

MY FAITH LEVEL   1 - 2 - 3 - 4 - 5 - 6 - 7 - 8 - 9 - 10

DATE

I AM ASKING GOD FOR

___

___

___

___

___

SCRIPTURES I AM STANDING ON

___

___

___

___

___

UPDATES

___

___

___

___

___

MY RESPONSE TO GOD'S ANSWER

___

___

___

___

___

So Jesus answered and said to them, "Have faith in God."
Mark 11:12

NOTES AND PICTURES

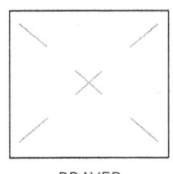
PRAYER ANSWERED

For where two or three are gathered together in My name, I am there in the midst of them.
Matthew 18:20

MY FAITH LEVEL   1 - 2 - 3 - 4 - 5 - 6 - 7 - 8 - 9 - 10

DATE

I AM ASKING GOD FOR
___
___
___
___
___
___

SCRIPTURES I AM STANDING ON
___
___
___
___
___
___

UPDATES
___
___
___
___
___
___

MY RESPONSE TO GOD'S ANSWER
___
___
___
___
___
___

So Jesus answered and said to them, "Have faith in God."
Mark 11:12

NOTES AND PICTURES

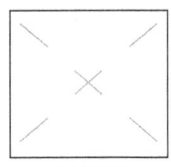

PRAYER ANSWERED

For where two or three are gathered together in My name, I am there in the midst of them.
Matthew 18:20

MY FAITH LEVEL 1 - 2 - 3 - 4 - 5 - 6 - 7 - 8 - 9 - 10

DATE

I AM ASKING GOD FOR
___
___
___
___
___
___

SCRIPTURES I AM STANDING ON
___
___
___
___
___
___

UPDATES
___
___
___
___
___
___

MY RESPONSE TO GOD'S ANSWER
___
___
___
___
___
___

So Jesus answered and said to them, "Have faith in God."
Mark 11:12

NOTES AND PICTURES

PRAYER
ANSWERED

For where two or three are gathered together in My name, I am there in the midst of them.
Matthew 18:20

MY FAITH LEVEL   1 - 2 - 3 - 4 - 5 - 6 - 7 - 8 - 9 - 10

DATE

I AM ASKING GOD FOR
___
___
___
___
___
___

SCRIPTURES I AM STANDING ON
___
___
___
___
___
___

UPDATES
___
___
___
___
___
___

MY RESPONSE TO GOD'S ANSWER
___
___
___
___
___
___

So Jesus answered and said to them, "Have faith in God."
Mark 11:12

NOTES AND PICTURES

PRAYER
ANSWERED

For where two or three are gathered together in My name, I am there in the midst of them.
Matthew 18:20

MY FAITH LEVEL   1 - 2 - 3 - 4 - 5 - 6 - 7 - 8 - 9 - 10

DATE

I AM ASKING GOD FOR

_____
_____
_____
_____
_____

SCRIPTURES I AM STANDING ON

_____
_____
_____
_____
_____

UPDATES

_____
_____
_____
_____
_____

MY RESPONSE TO GOD'S ANSWER

_____
_____
_____
_____
_____

So Jesus answered and said to them, "Have faith in God."
Mark 11:12

NOTES AND PICTURES

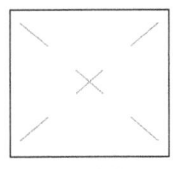
PRAYER ANSWERED

For where two or three are gathered together in My name, I am there in the midst of them.
Matthew 18:20

MY FAITH LEVEL   1 - 2 - 3 - 4 - 5 - 6 - 7 - 8 - 9 - 10

DATE

I AM ASKING GOD FOR
_____
_____
_____
_____
_____
_____

SCRIPTURES I AM STANDING ON
_____
_____
_____
_____
_____
_____

UPDATES
_____
_____
_____
_____
_____
_____

MY RESPONSE TO GOD'S ANSWER
_____
_____
_____
_____
_____
_____

So Jesus answered and said to them, "Have faith in God."
Mark 11:12

NOTES AND PICTURES

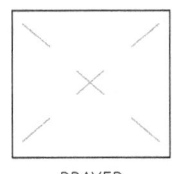

PRAYER
ANSWERED

For where two or three are gathered together in My name, I am there in the midst of them.
Matthew 18:20

MY FAITH LEVEL 1 - 2 - 3 - 4 - 5 - 6 - 7 - 8 - 9 - 10

DATE

I AM ASKING GOD FOR

_____
_____
_____
_____
_____
_____

SCRIPTURES I AM STANDING ON

_____
_____
_____
_____
_____
_____

UPDATES

_____
_____
_____
_____
_____
_____

MY RESPONSE TO GOD'S ANSWER

_____
_____
_____
_____
_____
_____

So Jesus answered and said to them, "Have faith in God."
Mark 11:12

NOTES AND PICTURES

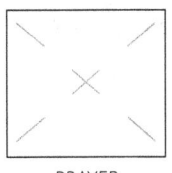

PRAYER ANSWERED

For where two or three are gathered together in My name, I am there in the midst of them.
Matthew 18:20

MY FAITH LEVEL   1 - 2 - 3 - 4 - 5 - 6 - 7 - 8 - 9 - 10

DATE

I AM ASKING GOD FOR

_____
_____
_____
_____
_____

SCRIPTURES I AM STANDING ON

_____
_____
_____
_____
_____

UPDATES

_____
_____
_____
_____
_____

MY RESPONSE TO GOD'S ANSWER

_____
_____
_____
_____
_____

So Jesus answered and said to them, "Have faith in God."
Mark 11:12

NOTES AND PICTURES

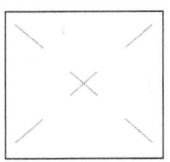
PRAYER ANSWERED

For where two or three are gathered together in My name, I am there in the midst of them.
Matthew 18:20

MY FAITH LEVEL   1 - 2 - 3 - 4 - 5 - 6 - 7 - 8 - 9 - 10

DATE

I AM ASKING GOD FOR
_____
_____
_____
_____
_____

SCRIPTURES I AM STANDING ON
_____
_____
_____
_____
_____
_____

UPDATES
_____
_____
_____
_____
_____

MY RESPONSE TO GOD'S ANSWER
_____
_____
_____
_____
_____

So Jesus answered and said to them, "Have faith in God."
Mark 11:12

NOTES AND PICTURES

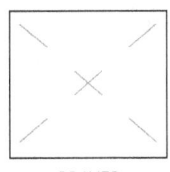

PRAYER
ANSWERED

For where two or three are gathered together in My name, I am there in the midst of them.
Matthew 18:20

MY FAITH LEVEL   1 - 2 - 3 - 4 - 5 - 6 - 7 - 8 - 9 - 10

DATE

I AM ASKING GOD FOR
___
___
___
___
___
___

SCRIPTURES I AM STANDING ON
___
___
___
___
___
___

UPDATES
___
___
___
___
___

MY RESPONSE TO GOD'S ANSWER
___
___
___
___
___

So Jesus answered and said to them, "Have faith in God."
Mark 11:12

NOTES AND PICTURES

PRAYER ANSWERED

For where two or three are gathered together in My name, I am there in the midst of them.
Matthew 18:20

MY FAITH LEVEL   1 - 2 - 3 - 4 - 5 - 6 - 7 - 8 - 9 - 10

DATE

I AM ASKING GOD FOR
___
___
___
___
___
___

SCRIPTURES I AM STANDING ON
___
___
___
___
___
___

UPDATES
___
___
___
___
___

MY RESPONSE TO GOD'S ANSWER
___
___
___
___
___
___

So Jesus answered and said to them, "Have faith in God."
Mark 11:12

NOTES AND PICTURES

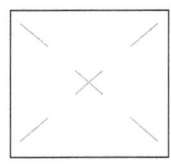

PRAYER
ANSWERED

For where two or three are gathered together in My name, I am there in the midst of them.
Matthew 18:20

MY FAITH LEVEL 1 - 2 - 3 - 4 - 5 - 6 - 7 - 8 - 9 - 10

DATE

I AM ASKING GOD FOR
_____
_____
_____
_____
_____
_____

SCRIPTURES I AM STANDING ON
_____
_____
_____
_____
_____
_____

UPDATES
_____
_____
_____
_____
_____
_____

MY RESPONSE TO GOD'S ANSWER
_____
_____
_____
_____
_____
_____

So Jesus answered and said to them, "Have faith in God."
Mark 11:12

NOTES AND PICTURES

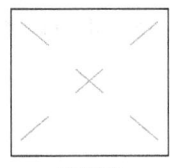

PRAYER
ANSWERED

For where two or three are gathered together in My name, I am there in the midst of them.
Matthew 18:20

MY FAITH LEVEL   1 - 2 - 3 - 4 - 5 - 6 - 7 - 8 - 9 - 10

DATE

I AM ASKING GOD FOR

_____
_____
_____
_____
_____

SCRIPTURES I AM STANDING ON

_____
_____
_____
_____
_____

UPDATES

_____
_____
_____
_____
_____

MY RESPONSE TO GOD'S ANSWER

_____
_____
_____
_____
_____

So Jesus answered and said to them, "Have faith in God."
Mark 11:12

NOTES AND PICTURES

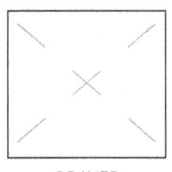

PRAYER ANSWERED

For where two or three are gathered together in My name, I am there in the midst of them.
Matthew 18:20

MY FAITH LEVEL   1 - 2 - 3 - 4 - 5 - 6 - 7 - 8 - 9 - 10

DATE

I AM ASKING GOD FOR
_____
_____
_____
_____
_____
_____

SCRIPTURES I AM STANDING ON
_____
_____
_____
_____
_____
_____

UPDATES
_____
_____
_____
_____
_____

MY RESPONSE TO GOD'S ANSWER
_____
_____
_____
_____
_____
_____

So Jesus answered and said to them, "Have faith in God."
Mark 11:12

NOTES AND PICTURES

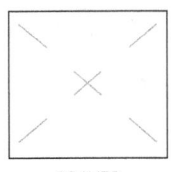

PRAYER
ANSWERED

For where two or three are gathered together in My name, I am there in the midst of them.
Matthew 18:20

MY FAITH LEVEL   1 - 2 - 3 - 4 - 5 - 6 - 7 - 8 - 9 - 10

DATE

I AM ASKING GOD FOR

_____
_____
_____
_____
_____
_____

SCRIPTURES I AM STANDING ON

_____
_____
_____
_____
_____
_____

UPDATES

_____
_____
_____
_____
_____
_____

MY RESPONSE TO GOD'S ANSWER

_____
_____
_____
_____
_____
_____

So Jesus answered and said to them, "Have faith in God."
Mark 11:12

NOTES AND PICTURES

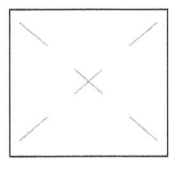
PRAYER ANSWERED

For where two or three are gathered together in My name, I am there in the midst of them.
Matthew 18:20

MY FAITH LEVEL   1 - 2 - 3 - 4 - 5 - 6 - 7 - 8 - 9 - 10

DATE

I AM ASKING GOD FOR

___

SCRIPTURES I AM STANDING ON

___

UPDATES

___

MY RESPONSE TO GOD'S ANSWER

___

So Jesus answered and said to them, "Have faith in God."
Mark 11:12

NOTES AND PICTURES

PRAYER
ANSWERED

For where two or three are gathered together in My name, I am there in the midst of them.
Matthew 18:20

MY FAITH LEVEL 1 - 2 - 3 - 4 - 5 - 6 - 7 - 8 - 9 - 10

DATE

I AM ASKING GOD FOR

SCRIPTURES I AM STANDING ON

UPDATES

MY RESPONSE TO GOD'S ANSWER

So Jesus answered and said to them, "Have faith in God."
Mark 11:12

NOTES AND PICTURES

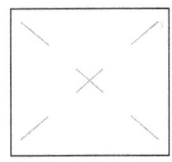

PRAYER ANSWERED

For where two or three are gathered together in My name, I am there in the midst of them.
Matthew 18:20

MY FAITH LEVEL   1 - 2 - 3 - 4 - 5 - 6 - 7 - 8 - 9 - 10

DATE

I AM ASKING GOD FOR

_____
_____
_____
_____
_____
_____

SCRIPTURES I AM STANDING ON

_____
_____
_____
_____
_____
_____

UPDATES

_____
_____
_____
_____
_____

MY RESPONSE TO GOD'S ANSWER

_____
_____
_____
_____
_____
_____

So Jesus answered and said to them, "Have faith in God."
Mark 11:12

NOTES AND PICTURES

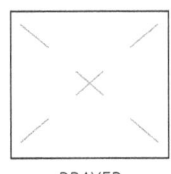

PRAYER ANSWERED

For where two or three are gathered together in My name, I am there in the midst of them.
Matthew 18:20

MY FAITH LEVEL   1 - 2 - 3 - 4 - 5 - 6 - 7 - 8 - 9 - 10

DATE

I AM ASKING GOD FOR
___
___
___
___
___
___

SCRIPTURES I AM STANDING ON
___
___
___
___
___
___

UPDATES
___
___
___
___
___

MY RESPONSE TO GOD'S ANSWER
___
___
___
___
___
___

So Jesus answered and said to them, "Have faith in God."
Mark 11:12

NOTES AND PICTURES

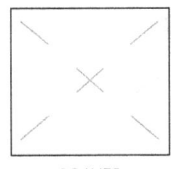

PRAYER ANSWERED

For where two or three are gathered together in My name, I am there in the midst of them.
Matthew 18:20

MY FAITH LEVEL   1 - 2 - 3 - 4 - 5 - 6 - 7 - 8 - 9 - 10

DATE

I AM ASKING GOD FOR
_____
_____
_____
_____
_____

SCRIPTURES I AM STANDING ON
_____
_____
_____
_____
_____

UPDATES
_____
_____
_____
_____
_____

MY RESPONSE TO GOD'S ANSWER
_____
_____
_____
_____
_____

So Jesus answered and said to them, "Have faith in God."
Mark 11:12

NOTES AND PICTURES

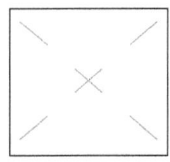

PRAYER
ANSWERED

For where two or three are gathered together in My name, I am there in the midst of them.
Matthew 18:20

SCRIPTURES TO STAND ON

HEALING

James 5:15 NKJV
15 And the prayer of faith will save the sick, and the Lord will raise him up. And if he has committed sins, he will be forgiven.

Jeremiah 33:6 NKJV
6 Behold, I will bring it health and healing; I will heal them and reveal to them the abundance of peace and truth.

Luke 8:50 NKJV
50 But when Jesus heard it, He answered him, saying, "Do not be afraid; only believe, and she will be made well."

Isaiah 41:13 NKJV
13 For I, the Lord your God, will hold your right hand,
Saying to you, 'Fear not, I will help you.'

James 5:14-16 NIV
14 Is anyone among you sick? Let them call the elders of the church to pray over them and anoint them with oil in the name of the Lord. 15 And the prayer offered in faith will make the sick person well; the Lord will raise them up.

Isaiah 58:8 NKJV
8 Then your light will break forth like the dawn, and your healing will quickly appear; then your righteousness will go before you, and the glory of the Lord will be your rear guard.

Matthew 4:23 NKJV
23 Jesus went throughout Galilee, teaching in their synagogues, proclaiming the good news of the kingdom, and healing every disease and sickness among the people.

Acts 10:38 NKJV
38 how God anointed Jesus of Nazareth with the Holy Spirit and power, and how he went around doing good and healing all who were under the power of the devil, because God was with him.

Isaiah 53:5 NKJV
5 But He was wounded for our transgressions, He was bruised for our iniquities; The chastisement for our peace was upon Him, And by His stripes we are healed.

FINANCE

Deuteronomy 28:6 NKJV
6 Blessed shall you be when you come in, and blessed shall you be when you go out.

Phillipians 4:19 NKJV
19 And my God shall supply all your need according to His riches in glory by Christ Jesus.

Job 22:21 NKJV
21 Now acquaint yourself with Him, and be at peace; Thereby good will come to you.

Proverbs 13:22 NKJV
22 A good man leaves an inheritance to his children's children,
But the wealth of the sinner is stored up for the righteous.

3 John 1:2 NKJV
Beloved, I pray that you may prosper in all things and be in health, just as your soul prospers.

2 Corinthians 9:7 NKJV
7 So let each one give as he purposes in his heart, not grudgingly or of necessity; for God loves a cheerful giver.

Deuteronomy 4:40 NKJV
40 You shall therefore keep His statutes and His commandments which I command you today, that it may go well with you and with your children after you, and that you may prolong your days in the land which the Lord your God is giving you for all time."

Psalm 112:3 NKJV
3 Wealth and riches will be in his house, And his righteousness endures forever.

Ecclesiastes 5:19 NKJV
19 As for every man to whom God has given riches and wealth, and given him power to eat of it, to receive his heritage and rejoice in his labor—this is the gift of God.

Isaiah 60:5 NKJV
5 Then you shall see and become radiant, And your heart shall swell with joy; Because the abundance of the sea shall be turned to you, The wealth of the Gentiles shall come to you.

RELATIONSHIP

Proverbs 10:12 NKJV
12 Hatred stirs up strife, But love covers all sins.

Romans 13:8 NKJV
8 Owe no one anything except to love one another, for he who loves another has fulfilled the law.

Galatians 5:22-23 NKJV
22 But the fruit of the Spirit is love, joy, peace, longsuffering, kindness, goodness, faithfulness, 23 [a]gentleness, self-control. Against such there is no law.

Ephesians 4:29 NKJV
29 Let no corrupt word proceed out of your mouth, but what is good for necessary [a]edification, that it may impart grace to the hearers.

Ephesians 5:2 NKJV
2 And walk in love, as Christ also has loved us and given Himself for us, an offering and a sacrifice to God for a sweet-smelling aroma.

1 Corinthians 13:4-7 NKJV
7 Love suffers long and is kind; love does not envy; love does not parade itself, is not [b]puffed up; 5 does not behave rudely, does not seek its own, is not provoked, [c]thinks no evil; 6 does not rejoice in iniquity, but rejoices in the truth; 7 bears all things, believes all things, hopes all things, endures all things.

Psalm 5:11 NKJV
11 But let all those rejoice who put their trust in You; Let them ever shout for joy, because You defend them; Let those also who love Your name Be joyful in You.

John 13:34 NKJV
34 A new commandment I give to you, that you love one another; as I have loved you, that you also love one another.

Romans 13:8 NKJV
8 Owe no one anything except to love one another, for he who loves another has fulfilled the law.

FORGIVENESS

Luke 6:37 NKJV
37 Judge not, and you shall not be judged. Condemn not, and you shall not be condemned. Forgive, and you will be forgiven.

1 Corinthians 13:4-5 NKJV
4 Love suffers long and is kind; love does not envy; love does not parade itself, is not [a]puffed up; 5 does not behave rudely, does not seek its own, is not provoked, [b]thinks no evil;

Ephesians 4:31-32 NKJV
31 Let all bitterness, wrath, anger, [a]clamor, and evil speaking be put away from you, with all malice. 32 And be kind to one another, tenderhearted, forgiving one another, even as God in Christ forgave you.

Mathew 6:14-15 NKJV
14 For if you forgive men their trespasses, your heavenly Father will also forgive you. 15 But if you do not forgive men their trespasses, neither will your Father forgive your trespasses.

Colossians 3:13 NKJV
13 Bearing with one another, and forgiving one another, if anyone has a complaint against another; even as Christ forgave you, so you also must do.

Matthew 6:12 NKJV
12 And forgive us our debts, as we also have forgiven our debtors.

Colossians 1:14 NKJV
14 In whom we have redemption through His blood, the forgiveness of sins.

Psalm 32:1 NKJV
1 Blessed is he whose transgression is forgiven, Whose sin is covered.

Psalm 106:1 NKJV
1 Praise the Lord! Oh, give thanks to the Lord, for He is good! For His mercy endures forever.

Mark 11:25 NKJV
25 And whenever you stand praying, if you have anything against anyone, forgive him, that your Father in heaven may also forgive you your trespasses.

Matthew 6:15 NKJV
15 But if you do not forgive men their trespasses, neither will your Father forgive your trespasses.

DIRECTION

John 14:6 NKJV
6 Jesus said to him, "I am the way, the truth, and the life. No one comes to the Father except through Me.

Acts 4:32 NKJV
32 Now the multitude of those who believed were of one heart and one soul; neither did anyone say that any of the things he possessed was his own, but they had all things in common.

1 Peter 3:15 NKJV
15 But [a]sanctify [b]the Lord God in your hearts, and always be ready to give a defense to everyone who asks you a reason for the hope that is in you, with meekness and fear;

Matthew 24:37-41 NKJV
37 But as the days of Noah were, so also will the coming of the Son of Man be. 38 For as in the days before the flood, they were eating and drinking, marrying and giving in marriage, until the day that Noah entered the ark, 39 and did not know until the flood came and took them all away, so also will the coming of the Son of Man be. 40 Then two men will be in the field: one will be taken and the other left. 41 Two women will be grinding at the mill: one will be taken and the other left.

Psalm 61 NKJV
61 Hear my cry, O God; Attend to my prayer. From the end of the earth I will cry to You, When my heart is overwhelmed; Lead me to the rock that is higher than I. For You have been a shelter for me, A strong tower from the enemy.

Psalm 23:3 NKJV
3 He restores my soul; He leads me in the paths of righteousness For His name's sake.

Psalm 5:8 NKJV
8 Lead me, O Lord, in Your righteousness because of my enemies; Make Your way straight before my face.

Psalm 31:3 NKJV
3 For You are my rock and my fortress; Therefore, for Your name's sake, Lead me and guide me.

Psalm 139:10 NKJV
10 Even there Your hand shall lead me, And Your right hand shall hold me.

PROSPERITY

Proverbs 15:6 NKJV
In the house of the righteous there is much treasure, but in the revenue of the wicked is trouble.

Matthew 6:33-34 NKJV
33 But seek first the kingdom of God and His righteousness, and all these things shall be added to you. 34 Therefore do not worry about tomorrow, for tomorrow will worry about its own things. Sufficient for the day is its own trouble.

Deuteronomy 28:13 NKJV
13 And the Lord will make you the head and not the tail; you shall be above only, and not be beneath, if you [a]heed the commandments of the Lord your God, which I command you today, and are careful to observe them.

Psalms 37:4 NKJV
4 Delight yourself also in the Lord, And He shall give you the desires of your heart.

Luke 6:38 NKJV
38 Give, and it will be given to you: good measure, pressed down, shaken together, and running over will be put into your bosom. For with the same measure that you use, it will be measured back to you.

Psalm 25:13 NKJV
13 He himself shall dwell in prosperity, And his descendants shall inherit the earth.

Psalm 35:27 NKJV
27 Let them shout for joy and be glad, Who favor my righteous cause; And let them say continually, Let the Lord be magnified, Who has pleasure in the prosperity of His servant.

Deuteronomy 8:18 NKJV
18 And you shall remember the Lord your God, for it is He who gives you power to get wealth, that He may establish His covenant which He swore to your fathers, as it is this day.

Proverbs 13:22 NKJV
22 A good man leaves an inheritance to his children's children, But the wealth of the sinner is stored up for the righteous.

ABOUT THE AUTHOR

David Harrelson is an ordained minister and a dynamic youth pastor for a growing church in Tulsa, Oklahoma. He has been actively involved in inner-city ministries for over 25 years. Together with his wife and children, he owns and operates Dads-Place Youth Ministries, a 70-acre weekend youth camp that offers extreme activities for disadvantaged and fatherless youth in the Tulsa area. This Christian-based, no-cost camp reaches at-risk kids through volunteer mentors who spend time doing outdoor activities like ATV riding, playing airsoft, fishing, archery, cooking over campfires, patriotic activities, and much more.

Dads-Place works directly with DHS and other child placement organizations to find forever families for Oklahoma's nearly 7,000 underprivileged and unplaced youth. You can learn more about Dads-Place at www.Dads-Place.org.

Apart from his ministry work, David is also an IT business professional, entrepreneur, and involved citizen. After graduating from Oklahoma State University, he developed software-based systems for numerous national and international companies. His software development has recovered over 150 million dollars for the airline industry. In 2001, David co-founded DATA3 Corporation in Tulsa, Oklahoma, taking his entrepreneurial leanings to a new level.

DATA3 has become a premier provider of data centers, professional IT services, and enterprise software development services. It is located in Tulsa, Oklahoma. You can learn more about DATA3 at www.datathree.com.

David is married and has nine children, three biological, four adopted, and currently two foster children.